RAW BACON FROM POLAND

Christina Masciotti

BROADWAY PLAY PUBLISHING INC
224 E 62nd St, NY, NY 10065
www.broadwayplaypub.com
info@broadwayplaypub.com

RAW BACON FROM POLAND
© Copyright 2017 Christina Masciotti

Cover photo by Maria Baranova

First edition: September 2017
I S B N: 978-0-88145-732-2

Book design: Marie Donovan
Page make-up: Adobe InDesign
Typeface: Palatino

RAW BACON FROM POLAND was first produced at the Abrons Arts Center at the Henry Street Settlement, opening on 1 June 2017. The cast and creative contributors were:

DENNIS .... Joel Perez
ALICE/WOMAN IN A HAT ....Kate Benson
MARCO/KEN ....Jay Smith
JOHN/FREDDY.................................Douglas Scott Streater
CUSTOMER...Paul Boocok
LITTLE GIRL .... Miah Velazquez/Isabella Lagares

Director.. Ben Williams
Set & costume design....................................Jacob A Climer
Lighting design .... Barbara Samuels
Sound design... Ben Williams
Stage manager..Oceana James
Assistant stage manager/
Child supervisor.. Deidrea Hamid
Production manager .... Ann Marie Dorr
Technical director...Carl Whipple
Assistant lighting designer/
Master electrician ....Dallas Estes
Sound assistant..Eric Bayless-Hall
Line producer .... Sandra Garnder, Lingua Franca Arts

CHARACTERS & SETTING

DENNIS, *Puerto Rican, shoe salesman, 20s, male, aspiring personal trainer, veteran*
ALICE, *social worker, 40s, female*
MARCO, *master shoe salesman, 40s, male*
JOHN, *rookie shoe salesman, 20s, male*
WOMAN IN HAT, *customer, no money, 60s, female*
CUSTOMER, *dripping with money, 40s, male*
FREDDY, *veteran mentor, 30s, male*
KEN, *counselor, 40s, male*
LITTLE GIRL, *dark hair, resembles* DENNIS, *6, female*
MAN IN FATIGUES/INSURGENT/ONE, *played by actor who plays* JOHN/FREDDY
MAN IN FATIGUES/INSURGENT/TWO, *played by actor who plays* ALICE/WOMAN IN HAT
MAN IN FATIGUES/INSURGENT/THREE *played by actor who plays* MALE CUSTOMER

MARCO/KEN *can also be played by the same actor*

ACT ONE: *Brooklyn Treatment Court, a luxury shoe store in Manhattan*

ACT TWO: *An inpatient rehab upstate, Brooklyn Treatment Court, a city park*

ACT ONE

Scene 1

(A cubicle in Brooklyn Treatment Court. DENNIS *and* ALICE *are seated.)*

ALICE: Tell me a little bit about why you're here.

DENNIS: I shouldn't be here. I shouldn't have took that plea. Any time a woman hits a man and calls the police, the man is arrested for domestic violence.

ALICE: What happened the day you were arrested?

DENNIS: It's wrong, it's wrong, it's wrong.

ALICE: Dennis, why am I meeting you here in Brooklyn Treatment Court?

DENNIS: When I was in Iraq, I was busting down doors and strangling people. If I wanted to strangle my wife, they woulda found her dead in the car.

ALICE: O K. Let's focus on one thing at a time. I want to make sure you have a successful outcome through this program. You've been ordered to treatment three times a week—

DENNIS: I gotta copay every time?

ALICE: Yes.

DENNIS: Jesus fucking Christ. Why!

ALICE: When you get medical treatment and your insurance covers it, you make a copayment. That's how insurance works.

DENNIS: I don't belong in that group! I don't have a problem with anger! I don't have a substance abuse issues. I'm not sure I even believe there's such a thing as a borderline personality disorder. And I'm insulted I have to sit in a room with a bunch of rastas who beat the shit outta they wives!

ALICE: What's it like for you to be in a group like that?

DENNIS: Fucking bowlshit.

ALICE: Sounds like you have a lot to be angry about.

DENNIS: Damn right I do. My wife pulled over and I grabbed her hair and her neck. That's it! Now I have to pay forty dollars three times a week? I work at a shoe store. I make minimal wage and commissions. I have a daughter.

ALICE: Treatment is expensive. It's also expensive if you're in jail and your rent's not being paid. I understand you're pissed, but you can't blow up at the front desk because you have to make a payment. Make the payments or tell your lawyer you can't comply with the terms of treatment. *(Pause)* Look, you agreed to an alternative to incarceration. We can't change why you're here. We can't change that you pled guilty. What's your goal while you're here?

DENNIS: My goal is to see my kid. I see her one day a week. I don't want less custody.

ALICE: O K, let's work on that.

Scene 2

(*A luxury shoe store.* JOHN, MARCO, *and* DENNIS *roam the floor.*)

JOHN: I can't believe I wasted my up on that crazy bitch.

MARCO: Watch out for women in hats. They never buy.

JOHN: But you said older women looking at men's shoes are a sure thing. They're on a mission.

MARCO: Not if they're wearing a giant purple hat.

DENNIS: This place is magnetic for bowlshit.

MARCO: Park Avenue Psychotherapy's at that corner. (*He points.*) The drugstore's there. (*He points to another corner.*) We're in between. That means loopy tunes on their way to picking up prescriptions pass through us.

JOHN: I don't think I'm cut out for this.

MARCO: You just started.

JOHN: I know. I like it here. The atmosphere is outgoing. But I hate feet.

MARCO: Get your multiples up, and see if you don't start loving 'em.

JOHN: Yeah, I don't have what you have.

MARCO: What do you mean?

DENNIS: He can't lie.

MARCO: Coming from the most dishonest fucker I know.

DENNIS: I only tell small lies. Elephant lies. White elephant lies.

JOHN: I think people can sense I'm desperate.

MARCO: Listen, this is what you have to do. When you go to the stockroom come back with four boxes:

what the customer wants, same style different color, same color different style, and the six hundred dollar version. Only give 'em one box. Let them ask you: "Are these all for me?" They will. Tell 'em you found a few similar ones in their size. They'll wanna try 'em. That's how you sell shoes. Arouse curiosity. People have the means to be convinced they want more than they need.

DENNIS: Papo, you a library in motion.

(DENNIS *lifts up his shirt and pulls* MARCO's *hand to his bare stomach.*)

MARCO: What the hell!

DENNIS: The last nena I had in here felt my bicep muscle. Only sale all week.

MARCO: You are a hhhhhhhuge pain in the ass!

DENNIS: Wow, Papo. You never moved your face like that since I met you. You looked like you lost your whole nervous system. You were like in thrombosis.

MARCO: Thank you for corrupting a nice gesture. I was trying to give useful advice.

DENNIS: Me, too. Sexability sells.

JOHN: Noted.

DENNIS: Look at me. I eat cookies before bed. Lots of cookies. And I still have muscular guts. They look fat, but they hard as rockets. I'm most proud of my butt. It sticks out, but it's harder than my thighs when I flex it.

MARCO: Next time Suski reams you out for your numbers, don't come running to me.

DENNIS: Papo, this job ain't the end for me. It's just a step. Fuck this one procent commission shit. When I'm a personal trainer, I'll be making sixty dollars an hour. That's my speed. I'm gonna change my whole physical repertoire. Buy one of those suburbian muckmansions. Off a big highway with mall strips. Five bedrooms,

four bathrooms. Golfing. Get my daughter back. Give
her the best of everything. For breakfast we'll have raw
bacon from Poland. I'll be running toward her with a
happy face and that shit not even on a fork. Right out
of my hands. We'll go on vacation to some part of the
world that has little monkeys that don't rip your face
off. Swimming in the ocean. With swimming things
that you lean on because they don't go down, they
float.

MARCO: You and your fabulous ass have it made.

Scene 3

(DENNIS *joins* ALICE *in her cube.*)

ALICE: You went to one out of three required group
sessions last week.

DENNIS: How's that group helping me? Telling me
I'm angry and my decisions ended me up there. No
shit, I'm angry. I'm in a domestic violence program
and I don't abuse my wife. The guy who runs it has an
earring in his tongue. Why should I listen to him? And
he never even asked me what happened, that's what
really boils me up.

ALICE: I get it. You don't feel heard.

DENNIS: I don't care if I'm heard or not, I just want it to
be over!

ALICE: You don't care? Then why are we talking?
Don't sit in that chair if you don't want to be heard. Go
to your fucking appointment on Thursday and stop
talking to me.

(*Pause*)

DENNIS: (*Quietly*) Ass early.

ALICE: What was that?

DENNIS: Shit's too early.

ALICE: You signed up for the morning session, so you could make it to your job on time.

DENNIS: I can't wake up that early.

ALICE: Why not?

DENNIS: I'm living with my grandmother. I don't know her that good. She's an olderly lady, eighty years old. It's a cluttered apartment. I don't have a room where I can close the door. She comes out and turns the T V on. Pito walks around at night.

ALICE: Your father lives there, too?

DENNIS: He's homeless. He's waiting to get housing through H R A.

ALICE: Must be hard to get a good night's sleep there.

DENNIS: Things keep getting my sleep worse and worse.

ALICE: When did you start having problems sleeping?

DENNIS: 2014.

ALICE: What happened in 2014?

DENNIS: Tikrit.

ALICE: Wanna tell me about that?

DENNIS: Nothing to tell.

ALICE: What do you do when you can't sleep?

DENNIS: I play video games.

ALICE: That help?

DENNIS: I don't know. I like the game called Gears of War. You play that?

ALICE: No.

DENNIS: It has good guys and bad guys. The good guys are soldiers, they trying to keep humanity alive. The bad guys are demons, they won't stop killing people in the area. I like the sound of the demon when you shoot 'em and they drop down, start screaming. I like that sound. When you coming in a place that has a lot of demons. When you hear that sound, get ready cause you gonna fight with a lot of demons!

ALICE: Do you ever drink when you can't sleep?

DENNIS: Sometimes. I used to sniff Percoset. Can't do that no more.

ALICE: You tested positive for alcohol.

DENNIS: I wasn't sanctioned for alcohol.

ALICE: Your sentence is twelve months of treatment - that's drug and alcohol free.

DENNIS: Why is the court so strict? I didn't drink any alcohol during the Pacquiao fight. I was positive four times last month and two times this month. That means I'm fifty procent better.

ALICE: No, that means you're two times closer to ninety days in rehab.

DENNIS: I never developed a tongue for wine. It's only to sleep. I can't do nothing else for relief of mind.

ALICE: By relief of mind, do you mean a coma? Because that's what combining alcohol and methadone will do for you. *(Pause)* There's an organization we work with that provides support to veterans in treatment.

DENNIS: I been to the V A. All they wanted to do was shove pills in my mouth.

ALICE: Not the V A. These are Iraq combat vets who work as mentors. I want you to meet them.

Scene 4

(The shoe store. Music plays. A WOMAN IN A HAT *browses the displays, eating almonds.* JOHN *does his best to avoid her.)*

WOMAN IN HAT: Why isn't anyone helping me? I been here ten minutes.

JOHN: How can I help you, Ma'am?

WOMAN IN HAT: You think I don't have money? I have money. My father drives a car. My father drives a millionaire car. My father's been a native New Yorker since 1941. My son lived and died in New York. I'm not lost in the city. I bet you have to ride the train to go home. You have a job, but you have to ride the train to go home.

JOHN: In fact, I do.

WOMAN IN HAT: These are eighty dollar boots. I'm goin for a job on Tuesday. Don't hire me Tuesday, I'm goin the fuck off. I don't care. I got food in the house. Fuck that. I get a check every month. I can say what I want. My mother gets forty-four thousand dollars a year for working security. My brother gets forty-two thousand. This phone is free. I don't have to pay rent on this phone. All these people pay thousands of dollars a month. I get two hundred and fifty minutes on Friday. These people don't have two hundred and fifty minutes. Look at this black card. I have that. Go get yours. It works, too.

JOHN: O K.

WOMAN IN HAT: You won't be gettin the money I'm gettin Friday. I been makin money since 1992. I had thousands last month. I get thousands and millions every two years. I still have time to go to the Social Security office and get S S I. Every two weeks they wanna know everything about me when I sign those papers.

(JOHN *turns off the lights and music.*)

WOMAN IN HAT: What's happening?

JOHN: Ma'am, there appears to be a power outage. I'm gonna have to ask you to leave for your own safety.

(*The* WOMAN IN HAT *exits.* JOHN *turns the lights back on.* DENNIS *stands in a doorway to the break room.*)

JOHN: Oh, man. Dennis. I didn't know how else to get rid of her. Please, don't tell Suski. He'll have my balls.

(JOHN *turns the music back on.*)

JOHN: This music isn't right. Why does Suski make us play this? It's too emotional.

(*With hand signals* DENNIS *motions for unseen people to either pass through the doorway or stop.*)

JOHN: (*Pause*) Dennis? What are you doing?

DENNIS: Stand back, Gonzalez. Camels on fire.

JOHN: Dennis. You O K?

DENNIS: They cut our power when they opened up on us.

JOHN: No, that was just me. You wanna sit down?

DENNIS: Who'll watch the door?

JOHN: They got it, Marine, you're good.

DENNIS: Did you see the little girl?

JOHN: What little girl?

DENNIS: She's losing too much blood. Where's Doc? Get Doc!

(JOHN *exits.*)

Scene 5

(ALICE's *cube.* FREDDY *enters.*)

FREDDY: Dave said you have a guy for us.

ALICE: I have a Marine vet. Two deployments. He's engaged with the court for a felony drug charge and a separate charge for domestic violence.

FREDDY: The charge was strangulation, right?

ALICE: I don't think I mentioned that.

FREDDY: Small world.

ALICE: I want to integrate him with the mentor program. I think he could make progress with a peer who's relatable.

FREDDY: Finally ready to admit you can't help vets?

ALICE: I'm sorry, is there a whole line of social workers waiting to talk to your guys? You think people are in a hurry to work with vets in Drug Court? To have the pleasure of sitting here and be treated like shit? To listen to people underreport their substance abuse and gloss over their criminal history? Damn. I'm taking someone's spot. A veteran who served with you wants to sit at my desk.

FREDDY: You got dental?

ALICE: Yeah, that I pay for.

FREDDY: Keep paying cause you'll be pickin up your teeth with broken fingers.

ALICE: Listen to me. No one wanted to take this guy. He was running his mouth and throwing chairs across the room. They were ready to transfer him to another court with no social workers. I'm taking care of him, but he needs more than a treatment plan. Will you work with me?

FREDDY: Does he have bad paper?

ALICE: His discharge was honorable.

FREDDY: If his discharge was dishonorable, he raped or murdered someone and he belongs in jail.

ALICE: You say that every time like I have a T B I. I was in art school while you were in bootcamp. You don't have to repeat yourself to me.

FREDDY: You may not have a T B I, but you have some kinda brain damage if you're a social worker. You work with junkies who'd rather be locked up. Leave the vets to me. Get me this guy's DD214 and I'll meet him Thursday.

Scene 6

(*The shoe store.* MARCO *builds a display.* DENNIS *enters.*)

DENNIS: Nice display. It looks like a shoe commercial.

MARCO: What?

DENNIS: It sounds like a shoe commercial.

MARCO: How?

DENNIS: You can see the person walking, and the shoes. Getting the shoes.

MARCO: I'm not asking any more questions.

DENNIS: I had a bad weekend, Papo.

MARCO: That's what happens when you're not cool.

DENNIS: I'm cool.

MARCO: No.

DENNIS: I'm loud cool.

MARCO: You're loud.

DENNIS: What are you talking about? I know exactly how to go about situations. It's not even like that. I'm not even talking about myself. My weekend was bad cause that bitch cancelled. She's the queen of switch and bait techniques. She'll tell you one thing, and do the complete other. I didn't see my daughter at all last week. She lost her first tooth. I missed all that. That goes against the court order. I'm supposed to have supervised visits with Essie through the whole divorce process.

MARCO: Sorry to hear that.

DENNIS: Well, you can't get mad at the whole world cause of one bad apple. I don't care what she does. She can go out with ten guys, just let me see my baby.

MARCO: She's seeing other guys already?

DENNIS: We did a whole woman's movement and she can't be alone for five minutes. She used to go to the store, the sleazy bags gather around her like she's a bee.

MARCO: People don't gather around bees.

DENNIS: Like she's a moth. She comes back, opens her foul mouth. Telling me, this guy loved me, that guy loved me. I was like: "You're very pretty. But you wear black the rest of your life, you look like witchcraft."

MARCO: She needs her self-esteem lifted and that's what you tell her?

DENNIS: I told her she's pretty. She needs to hear it every day, from every body, and repeat it all back to me. Not to make me jealous. To know what I had. Without that bitch, you know what I'd have? I'd have a house with money in the bank to fix it.

MARCO: You hear anything from Suski?

DENNIS: No. Why? He fuck up our checks again?

MARCO: John told Suski something happened here the other day. He said he had to shut down the store.

DENNIS: That had nothing to do with me.

MARCO: He said you were ranting about camels and a medic.

DENNIS: O K. His sales should be picking up soon cause he's learning how to lie then.

MARCO: What happened?

DENNIS: Nothing. I came up from my break. It was dark. It was quiet. I smelled almond nuts. That set me off. There was almond nuts in the air over there.

MARCO: Word from the wise: take care of your shit. Suski doesn't need a reason to fire you.

Scene 7

(ALICE *and* DENNIS *in her cube.*)

ALICE: How's your anxiety today?

DENNIS: My anxiety's bad. I want you to tell me my results.

ALICE: They're not in yet. And now your face is turning purple. (*Pause*) You understand your treatment is contingent upon program compliance.

DENNIS: That mean I gotta talk about my anxiety? I told you it's bad!

ALICE: O K. You don't have to talk about anything. I know you're putting up with a lot right now. You wanna sit here silently and wait for your results, we can do that.

(*Pause*)

DENNIS: (*Glancing around her cube*) I can't believe you got Coke bottles with your name on 'em. You found "Alice" in Duane Reade?

ALICE: No. Pennsylvania. I'm from there.

DENNIS: Pennsylvania? You Amish?

ALICE: What gave it away?

DENNIS: That's hardcore, the Amish. No electricity. No velcro. No buttons. I never seen Amish people till I traveled. I used to work for an inventory company. *(As he speaks tears start streaming down his cheeks, but his face is frozen. He seems unaware that he's crying.)*

ALICE: Dennis? What is it?

DENNIS: My old job. I used to go to different companies. Taking inventory. I didn't think the Amish existed because of the simple fact, they had they own community.

ALICE: *(Handing him a box)* Here are tissues.

DENNIS: I'm good.

ALICE: Dennis, you're crying.

(DENNIS touches his face. He takes a tissue and wipes his face.)

DENNIS: Those are nice tissues.

ALICE: Take as many as you want. Go ahead.

(DENNIS doesn't take any more. The tears have stopped. He stares off stoically.)

ALICE: Dennis, I don't want you to deny how you feel right now. The more you tell me, the better I can advocate for you.

DENNIS: Child Services took my daughter.

ALICE: Oh dear. Do you know the circumstances?

DENNIS: My wife's ma lives down the block. They do heroin together because of they mental being. There's some black history in the family.

ALICE: What does that mean?

DENNIS: There's suicides in her family. I'm guessing that has something to do with how fucked they are. It all went down on April 1st. Buncha fools exactly what they are.

ALICE: O K. I know this isn't what you expected, but we'll find a way.

DENNIS: Are you telling me something like: it's bad news then it's gonna be good news?

ALICE: No, it's all bad news. But I'm glad you're here when this happened. We can help you.

DENNIS: You can help me get my daughter back?

ALICE: We can support you as you go though the process.

DENNIS: Can you write a letter saying I'm a model court citizen and I don't have a drug problem?

ALICE: No.

DENNIS: Just say as less as possible. When they take a statement they always say to the best of your knowledge. You can leave a lot out.

ALICE: That's not how it works.

DENNIS: I'm requesting a date for the judge to hear my case. It don't look good that I'm in treatment court. I don't have a place to live. I threw my sister down the steps and she'll never let me live it down. You gotta do something.

ALICE: Let's go meet Freddy.

Scene 8

(FREDDY and DENNIS *walk together across the stage.*)

FREDDY: Semper Fi.

DENNIS: Oohrah.

FREDDY: How's it going?

DENNIS: Good, man.

FREDDY: You don't sound like it.

DENNIS: I ran outta exclamation marks.

FREDDY: How can I help?

DENNIS: It's my daughter's birthday next week. I was gonna take her on a ferry boat to Staten Island. She never been on a boat. It's free. She deserves every thing. She deserves every fucking thing.

FREDDY: Are you not allowed to take her?

DENNIS: They only let me see her in the foster care center.

FREDDY: You got a good lawyer?

DENNIS: Yeah. He walks the walk and talks weird. I'll sic him on 'em.

FREDDY: Whatever you gotta do, it won't be as hard as what you did over there.

DENNIS: That don't really take the ease off of it. I try to get off my pity party and grow over it. But I can't stop thinking about that whole shit that happened. I just go through the whole little scenery in my mind. Like it keeps happening.

FREDDY: You gotta keep busy. You in school?

DENNIS: I went to a three week class in Florida.

FREDDY: Where did you study?

DENNIS: On the calculator.

FREDDY: What did you study on the calculator?

DENNIS: I don't remember. I'm not one of these perfect students. Sit behind a desk till my ass is sore.

FREDDY: Is there anything you want to study?

DENNIS: Weightlifting. I wanna get into Bally's.

FREDDY: O K. I'll look into certification programs. You're eligible for benefits, so that could help. Hang in there, buddy. Hooah. *(He exits.)*

Scene 9

(The shoe store floor is covered with open shoe boxes and crumpled tissue paper. DENNIS seems to be making more of a mess cleaning it up. MARCO enters and stares at the mess in disbelief. JOHN is by the register, amused.)

JOHN: Dennis tried to help three people at once.

DENNIS: Bunch of middle country rednecks. All they bought was a belt.

MARCO: There's a lesson in this for you, John: Don't destroy half the sales floor for a belt.

JOHN: *(Laughing)* Oh, I learn a lot from Dennis every day.

DENNIS: What are you laughing at, Bambi?

JOHN: Nothing.

DENNIS: You double-faced piece of shit.

JOHN: Wait. Am I a marked man because I was laughing?

DENNIS: I know what you told Suski. I'm not the reason you had to shut down the store.

JOHN: I never said you were.

DENNIS: You don't have to backpaddle. I know what you said.

JOHN: Look, I don't know what you heard, but I didn't mean to blame you for anything. I freaked out. Well, to be honest, you freaked out, a bunch of times, and your freaking out started to freak me out. I told Suski out of genuine concern for you. I thought he could hook you up with some help.

(*A* MALE CUSTOMER *enters.*)

MARCO: Bambi, you're up.

(JOHN *approaches* MALE CUSTOMER.)

JOHN: Let me know if you have any questions, Sir.

MALE CUSTOMER: Thanks. (*He browses, stopping at a shoe.*)

JOHN: That's a beautiful shoe. Made in Brazil. The leather's a little stiff.

MALE CUSTOMER: Can I see it in an 11?

JOHN: Sure. (*He exits and returns with five boxes.*) Here's your 11.

MALE CUSTOMER: Cool. (*He tries it on.*)

JOHN: How's that?

MALE CUSTOMER: Feels great.

(MALE CUSTOMER *takes it off, and starts putting his own shoes back on.* JOHN *tries to get him to notice the other boxes.*)

JOHN: I also brought you these.

MALE CUSTOMER: I'm good.

JOHN: Are you sure you wouldn't like to try this one? It's made in Italy and the leather is much more supple.

MALE CUSTOMER: No, thanks. I know what to buy on-line now. (*He exits.*)

DENNIS: Good work, Bambi.

Scene 10

(DENNIS *approaches* ALICE'*s cube.*)

ALICE: What are you doing here? We don't have an appointment.

DENNIS: Miss Alice, I wanted to apologize about yesterday. Melvin was an asshole. He wouldn't tell me my results. He just said, "You got somethin to tell me?" I was like, "What? I'm clean. Let's go. The judge'll be proud." He goes: "Not what this says!"

ALICE: That doesn't sound like an apology.

DENNIS: Miss, people were yelling at me for no reason.

ALICE: Where do you think you are? This is a criminal justice building.

DENNIS: I wish for one minute you coulda been here to see what they did.

ALICE: If you would've come yesterday when we had an appointment, we could've talked all about this. Instead you tested positive, threw a fit, and ran out like the building was on fire.

DENNIS: I was so pissed I had to cop to taking Tylenol 4, but the judge was about to put me in jail. I just took a chance.

ALICE: You can tell me you're pissed. What you did made you look like a threat to your own well-being.

DENNIS: I tried to control myself, Miss Alice. I wanted to scream.

ALICE: They didn't take you out in bracelets, I know you controlled yourself.

DENNIS: You believe me that it was a false positive?

ALICE: I believe there is such a thing.

DENNIS: Why would I take heroin if I was on methadone? I won't get high. I could only get high from cocaine which I did NOT test positive for.

ALICE: Cup tests are unreliable. I want to believe you.

DENNIS: You don't? Miss Alice, I was tested the day before, I was negative. Heroin stays in your system for days. It's not possible I could be positive the next day.

ALICE: The important thing is, the judge gave you a shot. He keeps giving you chances. But the next consequence is inpatient treatment for ninety days. Don't make a mess in that toxicology next week.

Scene 11

(ALICE *approaches* FREDDY's *desk.*)

ALICE: Have you seen Dennis? He didn't show up today.

FREDDY: Saw him Tuesday.

ALICE: You did? How was he?

FREDDY: Good. I'm trying to keep him away from his brother.

ALICE: His brother?

FREDDY: His brother's selling guns in the projects. And he reported he stopped taking his medication.

ALICE: Dennis stopped taking his medication?

FREDDY: Yeah.

ALICE: Why didn't you tell me right away?

FREDDY: I'm on it. I'm looking into certificate programs for him. He needs to keep his mind occupied. He just needs something to look forward to.

ALICE: He's not stable enough to be in school right
now. Look, you need to be completely transparent
about what he tells you. He trusts you.

FREDDY: There's a reason he trusts me.

ALICE: And there's a reason he doesn't trust me. I'm
connected with the court. He's going to hide things
from me that he doesn't want going up the chain. He
presents as stable to me, but he's off his medication
doing who knows what. I didn't know his brother was
selling guns in the projects. If he harms himself, or
anyone else, there're big problems, O K? My license is
attached.

FREDDY: Well, I was thinking about what's best for him.

ALICE: And, of course, only you could know what's
best for him cause you were both in Fallujah at the
same fucking time.

FREDDY: He wasn't in Fallujah.

ALICE: I don't care where he was. Your "brotherhood"
cannot supercede his treatment. He should have been
remanded last week. He wasn't. Based on the only
evidence I had. You vouched for him. You put him in
danger.

FREDDY: It's not as bad as you're making it sound.

ALICE: You have no clue. You get angry when warrants
are issued. The arrest is what saves them. The arrest
would have been clinically appropriate for someone
medically unstable.

FREDDY: I didn't do anything wrong.

ALICE: You didn't do anything wrong, you just don't
know what you're doing!

FREDDY: O K. And if you did, why'd you come to me in
the first place?

ALICE: I'm talking about sticking to the limits of the fucking role! You answer the phone 24/7, ready to mobilize. Drive three hours to Jersey in the middle of the night to talk to a guy outside a diner. Walk him to an ambulette. Whatever it takes. You go off half-cocked, like a cowboy trying to heal yourself! That's the problem with veterans at risk monitoring veterans at risk. They're not clinicians attached to the court with licenses at stake! *(She exits.)*

Scene 12

(The shoe store. JOHN *mans the register while* MARCO *waits for a customer.* DENNIS *enters with a large box.)*

JOHN: Whatcha got there, Dennis?

DENNIS: See my middle finger on this box. Fuck you.

JOHN: What?

DENNIS: Suski took me off the floor and put me on socks.

MARCO: Ouch.

JOHN: I don't get it.

MARCO: *(Reaching into* DENNIS' *box, and holding out two pairs of socks)* Which one's black and which one's blue?

JOHN: They look identical.

MARCO: Exactly. Mix 'em up, and you'll catch hell. You have to check the numbers: black is A131480 and navy's A135480. You'll go blind checking those numbers all day. Then you have the perennials, the seasonals, the cotton, the wool, the silk, the liners, the anklets. They all have to be represented in the display, and kept segregated.If you don't lose your mind keeping the calf-length separate from the knee-length, you'll lose it keeping the toes tucked together, and the elastic side folded over in thirds. And where do we keep the extras? In a locked drawer right under the accessories like we do with the tassels, and the shoelaces, and the wallets, and the smart-thing cases? No. We keep them in one stockroom down two flights, and another stockroom four flights down and a block away via a maze of hallways. Yeah, you don't wanna be assigned to socks.

JOHN: Damn. Good thing Dennis already lost his mind.

DENNIS: You think this is a joke? It's my life, asshole!

(DENNIS *takes a knee-length sock out of the box and wraps it around* JOHN's *neck.*)

MARCO: Dennis, what are you doing!

(DENNIS *hauls* JOHN *across the floor, by his neck.*)

MARCO: Let go, Dennis! He can't breathe!

(DENNIS *is not listening.*)

MARCO: Stop! It's not worth it! Let go!

(DENNIS *backs away, and* JOHN *doubles over.*)

DENNIS: I was just playing.

JOHN: *(Whispering)* Marco, call the police

MARCO: Everything's cool now.

JOHN: I'm gonna call the police.

DENNIS: What do you mean you're gonna call the police? I said I was just playing.

JOHN: You assaulted me! *(He gets out his phone and swipes the screen.)*

DENNIS: You're gonna call the police on a guy wearing a suit? That ain't right.

(JOHN *dials three digits, puts the phone to his ear and exits.*)

DENNIS: Call the police! I am the police. My whole
family's police. Call 'em. How you doin today, officer?
Imma call the police on you.

(Blackout)

END OF ACT ONE

ACT TWO

Scene 1

(The rehab; shabby drywall panels line the perimeter.
DENNIS enters and finds KEN waiting.)

KEN: You Dennis?

DENNIS: Yes. Being that you know who I am, and I
don't know who you are, I must be pretty important.

KEN: Have a seat, Dennis. My name is Ken Higgins.
I'm the Counseling Coordinator here. Do you have
your Patient Handbook?

DENNIS: This thing?

KEN: Turn to page twelve, please, so we can review
our program policies and expectations. Can you read
number one out loud to me?

DENNIS: I did already on the train up here.

KEN: I'd like to go over a few things together to make
sure there're no misunderstandings.

DENNIS: You think I'm slow?

KEN: No, but it's interesting that you raise that. We
should explore that when we have more time together.
For now, could you please read number one?

DENNIS: Number One: Participate in individual and
group counseling sessions as applic-able.

KEN: Applicable.

DENNIS: Don't correct me from over there. I can read.

KEN: Your breathing is getting shallow, Dennis. What do you feel right now?

DENNIS: Nothing.

KEN: Nothing's not a feeling.

DENNIS: I feel like I'm wasting my time.

KEN: If I just looked at your body I'd say you feel agitated.

(DENNIS *freezes.*)

KEN: Don't freeze. You're allowed to feel agitated. I just want you to notice that. Even noticing agitation can lead you to new responses—instead of the automatic reactions that have become a habit.

DENNIS: I'm living paycheck to mouth. I'm stuck here, I could be working.

KEN: I want you to be working, Dennis. But you can't recover if you ignore what got you here. Whatever you avoid only increases your vulnerability to it. Whether that's feelings, memories, or aches and pains. You need to be aware of it to do something about it.

DENNIS: Can I go to my room now? That train ride got my head bad. I need to go to bed.

(Nightmare 1)

(DENNIS *walks downstage. We hear the sound of the screaming demon from his video game. The lights change.* WOMAN IN HAT *enters.*)

WOMAN IN HAT: You hear about Elmo?

DENNIS: Who's Elmo?

WOMAN IN HAT: Elmo came from China to kill the babies.

DENNIS: From Sesame Street?

WOMAN IN HAT: He came from China and he's killing the babies. Like you.

(WOMAN IN HAT *exits.* DENNIS *follows her for a few steps, changes directions, and punches a hole into a drywall panel. The lights change. He appears to awaken with a jolt.*)

Scene 2

(FREDDY *visits* DENNIS *in a common area.*)

DENNIS: I thought I walked into Someone Flew Over the Cuckoo's Nest. They have us drawing pictures in pyramids, our life ten years ago, knowing how far life is, you're here today and gone today. I can't take three months sitting in these rap sessions.

FREDDY: Give it a chance.

DENNIS: We have to get up at seven A M to seize the day. Siege the day. Whatever the day. They have us sitting around on these ratchet couches. Like a cult of Hohova witnesses or something. When people stand up to talk, the couches are so old, they fart. That's exactly what it sounds like. The air conditioner shoots out ice. You hear a crack and ice goes flying across the room. No one says shit. They're all kissing the sorry ass of that Counselor Ken. He has no idea what he's doing. Mr Egotistic. Someone asked where he lived and he said, "I don't feel comfortable sharing that." He thinks we need to follow him home to kill him? I'll slit his throat right outside this building.

FREDDY: Anger management is turning you around already.

DENNIS: Anger management is a coloring book. They gave me a box of pencils and a book called: Coloring the Mandela. Do you know mandelas? It's a circle. You fill up the circle with the little things. I think Leonardo Da Vinci was invented by that.

FREDDY: By what?

DENNIS: You know Leonardo Da Vinci?

FREDDY: Yeah.

DENNIS: He wasn't just a artist. He was a strong man. He could bent horseshoes with his bare hands.

FREDDY: I think that says more about the metallurgy of the time.

DENNIS: Anyway, some mandela artists are good. Those things are sold in galleries. But they use it to help the brain of a person with a nervous thing. Focusing on tiny details. They say, "Start coloring". They give me a coloring book to cure me, and they think I'm sick.

FREDDY: How you been sleeping?

DENNIS: Shitty, or not at all.

FREDDY: When I was brand fresh out of Fallujah, I had nightmares. Still do. Intense ones. Screws up your nights and days.

DENNIS: About what?

FREDDY: It's the same thing every time. I'm patrolling Highway 10 and a sniper cuts down my gunnery sergeant. He's screaming for his life. We have to leave him. *(Pause)* When I look back, he's on fire. Kids in flip flops are stomping on him. He's looking right at me, talking through the flames.

DENNIS: What's he saying?

FREDDY: He says he's going back to Delaware Tech to finish his degree.

(Tears stream down DENNIS' *blank face. Again, he seems unaware that he's crying.)*

FREDDY: Hey. It's my nightmare, not yours.

(DENNIS *is frozen.*)

FREDDY: Dennis, you O K?

DENNIS: Yeah, man.

FREDDY: Something flashed through your mind. Tell me. I been there.

(*Pause*)

DENNIS: I just miss my daughter.

(FREDDY *exits.*)

(Nightmare 2)

(*We hear the sound of the screaming demon from the video game. The lights change. A* LITTLE GIRL*'s face appears in the hole* DENNIS *punched into the drywall. She comes out from behind the wall in a sundress and flip flops, carrying a basket of flowers. She approaches him, smiling and reaching into the basket. She throws a flower at him.*)

DENNIS: Hey!

(DENNIS *picks it up. It's not a flower. It's a hypodermic needle. The* LITTLE GIRL *giggles, and continues to pelt him with needles.*)

DENNIS: (*With a sudden threatening move*) Get outta here!

(*The* LITTLE GIRL *exits.*)

Scene 3

(DENNIS *returns to* ALICE *in her cube.*)

ALICE: How are you adjusting to life in the treatment center?

DENNIS: It's an inconvenience to my privacy.

ALICE: What do you mean by that?

DENNIS: Guy who runs it is a dick. He doesn't qualify to be a leader type person. All rehab consists of is sitting around. It's all about the greed for money. Junkies go in, money comes out. That's how it works. It's mathematics. They're not perspective to our needs in there. Think the court will make me do nintey days?

ALICE: Yes.

DENNIS: You know. I'm willing to do twenty-eight.

ALICE: The court mandated you to a ninety day program.

DENNIS: I can't do ninety. I didn't think I'd get the whole ninety.

ALICE: You almost got the whole Rikers. I fought to keep you out.

DENNIS: I have to find another job. I can't be in some rehab for three months.

ALICE: We tried outpatient. It didn't work. You'll do nienty days inpatient. If you get in trouble again, your treatment will be extended.

DENNIS: I wasn't getting in trouble all the time. I was minding my own business till Bambi threw me under the school bus. You can't just do that and get away free of nothing.

ALICE: I see you're just getting off contract for unauthorized cell phone use.

DENNIS: That's the father I am. My daughter needed to talk to me. If I have to do a little ten day contract cleaning toilets cause of that, that's O K.

ALICE: How was your last visit with her? Your lawyer mentioned he set up a home visit with her foster parents.

DENNIS: The foster parents with the blonde hair, blue eyes?

ALICE: What did you think of them?

DENNIS: They rich white people. *(Pause)* I never lived nowhere that nice. Essie's well fed. Too much fed. Her skin cleared up. Her skin was all bloody. She was scratching, touching her clothes, getting blood all over the place. She had MRSA. Her mother swore up and down there was nothing you could do about it. Tried everything. But they straightened her skin out.

ALICE: That's good. Did you have fun with her?

DENNIS: She taught me how to play chess. She's actually good, she gets into it. I'm just trying to remember what the fuck I'm allowed to do. Chess ain't like anything goes. It's a challenge. You got two bishops, eight ponds, two rucks, two horses, the queen and king, all in battle afraid of they lives. They all got special moves. The ponds go straight in the beginning. After that, you eat your opponent's pieces sideways. The bishop goes diagonal, the ruck goes up and down, and the horses jump. The queen is the most powerful. It can go anywhere in the board. The king can only eat, and go one space, but he must be protected at all times. Or if not, he'll be checkmate. I heard checkmate so many times I almost flipped the board.

ALICE: Sounds like a great visit.

DENNIS: I'm split-minded on it. I think they're filling her head about me.

ALICE: What makes you say that?

DENNIS: I hugged her and she didn't hug me back. Like she knows I'm bad.

ALICE: I wouldn't jump to that conclusion. She's bounced around a lot, she's living with strangers, and she's very young. There's a lot she doesn't understand.

But she knows you're her dad, and you're spending time with her. That's more than I can say for a lot of the fathers who sit in that chair.

DENNIS: I got a lot going for me, but I just got one little problem behind it. I don't have stable housing and employment. That's what the judge wants to see.

ALICE: Stay the path, Dennis. You'll get there. First you have to move to the next phase of treatment.

Scene 4

(DENNIS *sits apprehensively in* KEN's *office.*)

KEN: Who did you feel safe with growing up?

DENNIS: Oh god. I can't answer that without a yoga ball. I have to be rolling around.

KEN: Now that you have that out of your system, can you answer the question?

DENNIS: Who'd I feel safe with? At home?

KEN: Yes.

DENNIS: Nobody.

KEN: What about outside the home? (*Pause*) Just think about it. Anyone come to mind?

(*Pause*)

DENNIS: The janitor at P S 24. He taught me how to lift weights in the mop room.

KEN: How do you feel when I say this: you are a good father.

DENNIS: Yoga ball time.

KEN: If you keep mentioning yoga we can switch to a yoga-based therapy.

DENNIS: God no.

KEN: It's one of the few treatments that's been shown to have a lasting impact on regulating P T S.

DENNIS: Don't do that to me. I'll run through the wall head first.

KEN: Then you have to stop fooling around. Respond honestly. There're no wrong answers. I'm just trying to raise your awareness of your body sensations. Can we continue?

(DENNIS *nods nervously.*)

KEN: How do you feel when I say you're a good father?

(*Pause*)

DENNIS: I feel a churning feeling.

KEN: Where?

DENNIS: In my chest. Like water moving. Like where my heart is. A kind of waterfall that goes in loops. And everything becomed swept up in it.

KEN: Take a deep breath. Allow your rib cage to expand. What happens to the feeling?

DENNIS: My shoulder feels tight.

KEN: What could explain that?

(DENNIS *appears lost in thought.*)

KEN: Dennis?

DENNIS: The digging.

KEN: You've been digging?

DENNIS: I don't want it to be too shallow. We have to be respective. (*He starts sobbing.*)

KEN: Stay with that, Dennis.

(DENNIS *tries to stop crying.*)

KEN: Don't stop.

DENNIS: No, no, no.

KEN: Dennis, notice what you're feeling. Just stand back. Watch.

(DENNIS *doubles over.*)

KEN: Sit up, Dennis.

(DENNIS *stays doubled over.*)

DENNIS: I can't do this.

KEN: You don't have to do anything. Just let the sensations pass through you.

DENNIS: They not passing, they ripping me the fuck up, you understand? (*He sits up.*)

KEN: O K. Notice how you feel now that you're sitting up. Notice how much your feelings can change with the slightest shift in your body.

DENNIS: I'm noticing my fist right now, you feel me?

KEN: Imagine that janitor here with you. If he could talk to you now, what would he say?

(*Pause*)

DENNIS: He'd tell me everybody got something under they table.

KEN: Plant your feet on the ground. Stand up.

(DENNIS *stands.*)

KEN: Breathe in, raise your arms up. Exhale, down.

(DENNIS *does so.*)

KEN: You proved it today. You can allow yourself to feel.

DENNIS: Usually when I feel like this I'm about to get arrested.

KEN: And no cops in sight. That's progress.

Scene 5

(ALICE *stops by* FREDDY's *desk.*)

ALICE: You've been visiting Dennis every week?

FREDDY: Yeah.

ALICE: Holy shit.

FREDDY: You're gonna tell me I'm overstepping?

ALICE: No. Isn't it like three hours to the facility?

FREDDY: Two and some change on MetroNorth.

ALICE: Wow.

FREDDY: What's your problem?

ALICE: No, it's just. How are you making it up there every week? I mean it's great. He needs the support. He's not in a military specific program. And he's reporting he feels like you're his friend. He looks forward to his visits with you. You're incentivizing his good behavior.

FREDDY: You're using those big words. I don't know what you're talking about.

ALICE: Oh, you're Army, I forgot.

FREDDY: Don't you have to go watch someone piss?

ALICE: I observed my toxicologies for the day. (*Pause*) Thank god it was a woman. Men, you have to watch it come out of the penis. They use wizzinators. Piss clear liquid and try to tell you they drank eight gallons of water. Women it's easy. You just have to look. Make sure there's no tube. One hand visible. One hand holding the cup. "Stop the stream. Go ahead." It's supposed to be mid-stream, but nobody gives a shit. The woman today had gas. Farting, farting, farting. "Oh girls, I'm embarrassed. I got gas. I'm sorry." Hershey squirt farting. "But I'm about to pee!" She had Kool-Aid all over her white shirt. I was like lady, I don't care what you do as long as I don't have to watch your dick.

FREDDY: I didn't need to hear any of that.

ALICE: Great, I just got much more pleasure out of telling you.

(FREDDY *starts to leave.*)

ALICE: Wait, Freddy. Thank you for your commitment to Dennis. It's making a big difference.

(FREDDY *exits.*)

Scene 6

(DENNIS *enters* ALICE's *cube smiling.*)

ALICE: You can't be Dennis Toledo.

DENNIS: Why not?

ALICE: You're smiling like a teddy bear, and Dennis fronts like he's something else.

DENNIS: That's how I am with the ladies.

ALICE: Since when?

DENNIS: I have good news.

ALICE: Get ready to ring that bell.

DENNIS: It's not worth the bell. I was walking on my way over here. There was a prescription pill bottle in the street. You know how pillheads are. We have to look at the bottle. See what it was. I left it there, kept walking.

ALICE: Ring that bell!

DENNIS: Yeah, yeah. I'm not ringing the bell.

ALICE: Congratulations on making it to the next phase of treatment.

DENNIS: I started talking at group. I had to give examples of how I been sneaky. Then whatever you say they ask you questions to see if you being honest, and you wanna change. I learned some things, too.

ALICE: Like what?

DENNIS: If you take opium for a long time you depend on it. And it slows down the opium your body produces. Then you have to take external opium. Methadone comes into play. Methadone is a synthetic opium you take to stop taking the real opium. Degenerates the nerve cells, that's what it does. But the unconscious will help you grow. That's where all the good stuff is about you, helps you be the opposite of what you doing now. Since I been in these groups, I read so many books, I'm shocked.

ALICE: You're reaping the rewards of all the hard work you're doing. The judge will be presenting you with red dog-tags at your next court appearance.

DENNIS: Thank you, Miss Alice. (*He gets up. On his way out, he slaps the bell.*) Order up!

Scene 7

(DENNIS *joins* KEN *in his office.*)

KEN: You've heard of rapid eye movements?

DENNIS: What. When you're scared?

KEN: No, it's what happens when you're sleeping— when you're dreaming in your deepest sleep. REM sleep is actually essential to healing. It's what helps you integrate your experiences into the past. Without it, all your past experiences stay unprocessed and raw.

DENNIS: Too bad I can't sleep.

KEN: The reason I bring it up is because it's possible to replicate what happens in REM sleep while still awake.

DENNIS: *(Holding out his wrists to be cuffed)* O K. I'm ready to do my time. Put me away.

KEN: Hear me out. All I'm going to do is move my index finger back and forth in front of your right eye. You're going to follow my finger while you bring a painful experience to mind. I know it sounds crazy, but it works. It has something to do with the movement of the eyes. And the memory is only the starting place. The focus is on activating associations. Just like would happen in a dream.

DENNIS: No disrespect to your education, but I'm not gonna sit here and go cross-eyed telling you about my experiences.

KEN: You don't have to tell me anything. You just have to be willing to remember.

DENNIS: I got no control over what I remember.

KEN: Good point. That's why we're doing this. So you can have control. This is how you get it.

DENNIS: I don't have to say anything?

KEN: Only what you feel comfortable saying. Whatever you want to keep to yourself, I don't need to know.

DENNIS: O K, I'll sit here.

KEN: You won't just sit there. It's O K. I thought you were ready to take this risk, I was wrong.

DENNIS: I'm ready, I'm ready.

KEN: I don't know if you can handle it.

DENNIS: Homie, I can handle whatever the fuck you want, but the more you talk about it, the more you pissing me off.

KEN: O K.

(KEN *moves his chair about four feet away from* DENNIS *and sits down.*)

KEN: Go to the memory you most want to block.

DENNIS: Fuck, man.

KEN: If you don't want to do this, now's the time back out.

DENNIS: I'm an adult. I don't back out.

KEN: No one is questioning that. Unclench your teeth. Breathe in, hold it, count to four. Exhale, six. Relax your hands. *(Pause)* Remember what you saw and heard. The smells. The sounds. The thoughts. Just let those moments come back. *(Pause)* Are you there?

DENNIS: I never fucking left.

KEN: How real does it feel on a scale of one to ten?

DENNIS: Maybe eight or nine.

KEN: Follow my finger. *(Moving his finger)* Deep breath. Notice what comes to mind.

(DENNIS' *breathing becomes rapid and shallow.*)

KEN: Keep tracking my finger. What are you thinking?

(*Three* MEN IN FATIGUES *appear behind* KEN *and* DENNIS. DENNIS *stands.*)

DENNIS: They everywhere.

KEN: Hold that image in your mind and keep watching my finger.

(KEN *does twenty more back and forth movements as if* DENNIS *is still seated.*)

KEN: Pay attention to what's on your mind now.

(DENNIS *and the* MEN *move in formation with hand signals.*)

DENNIS: My wife. She's running out of the house with Essie. I don't know what I did.

KEN: Stay there.

(KEN *does twenty more movements. The* MEN *drop on all fours and* DENNIS *rolls onto their collective back.*)

DENNIS: I'm driving a Humvee. I parked on a hill. I don't know how to put it in reverse to get it off the hill. I'm a target. Essie's in the back playing chess. What's she doing there? It's a war zone.

KEN: What are you doing?

DENNIS: I have to lay on top of her. To protect her. But she's suffocating. It's not working. She pushes me away.

(DENNIS *rolls onto the floor, and lies there. The* MEN *extend their hands to help him up.*)

KEN: What do you feel in your body?

DENNIS: I feel peaceful. Essie's saying, "It's O K".

(*Now that* DENNIS *is back on his feet the* MEN *appear to be circling him. They assume fighting stances.* DENNIS *begins to dodge blows left and right.*)

KEN: Feel the weight of your feet on the ground.

(*A three-on-one round of boxing continues with* DENNIS *at the center, fighting for his life.*)

KEN: Dennis, come back into the room. You're safe in the chair.

(DENNIS *battles his way to the chair, and slumps, as if retreating to his corner.*)

KEN: What do you feel now?

DENNIS: I don't know. (*Pause*) I guess I feel like I'm alive. I survived.

KEN: Excellent work, Dennis.

DENNIS: That's it?

KEN: For now. Watch for any differences in your general disposition over the next week. Particularly your ability to sleep through the night.

(Nightmare 3)

(We hear the sound of the screaming demon. The lights change. WOMAN IN HAT enters. DENNIS pulls out a machine gun. He aims it at her. She presses a button on her thigh and streaks of water soak her pants. He walks over to her and pulls down her pants. Her leg is strapped with a contraption that actors wear to pretend they've wet themselves on stage. She unstraps it from her leg, and gives it to him.)

WOMAN IN HAT: I brought this for you, so you can finally pass your drug screenings. *(She pulls up her pants, and exits.)*

DENNIS: Why, Mami? I'm clean! *(He throws it after her.)*

Scene 8

(FREDDY visits DENNIS in the common area.)

DENNIS: Essie's gonna have a fist for Thanksgiving.

FREDDY: A what?

DENNIS: You know when they eat a lot. She said she's having a nice soido Thanksgiving. Soido turkey. What the fuck is soido?

FREDDY: I think it's tofu.

DENNIS: My Thanksgiving will be in an insanity room. They're crimping. They're limping. They're eating deep fried chicken. Ice cream. Donuts. Looking at you with an open mouth full of mash potatoes. I wanna buy something where I don't see my periphereal vision.

FREDDY: Just eat by yourself and finish studying on the computer. How far did you make it through that book I got you?

DENNIS: The personal training shit? I flipped through it.

FREDDY: Did you take any practice tests?

DENNIS: They're on the computer.

FREDDY: I thought they had computers in the back here.

DENNIS: But you can't download or print nothing.

FREDDY: You don't need to.

DENNIS: Oh, shit. I should take some practice tests. All I been doing is entering sweepstakes. Since my grandmother died I won so far: a Pepperidge Farm wallet, a "Got Milk?" T-shirt. My grandma's working overtime.

FREDDY: Your application for Education Benefits came through. You're eligible for tuition assistance and certification test reimbursement. When you're ready we can sign you up for the real test.

Scene 9

(Group. Four chairs are pushed downstage. DENNIS, and three group members take their seats. KEN stands behind them.)

KEN: Let's do a check in. How was your week?

(They all start speaking at the same time. No words are decipherable until KEN holds a microphone before One.)

ONE: I saw my wife. She spent ten days on Rikers. She was selling no tax cigarettes. She got caught up in it.

Hers had the sticker. It was counterfeit stickers. New
York State stickers. Our garage was piled up with
cartons of cigarettes. She sold loosies for three dollars.
Jeans she went in with she had to wear ten days. She
was crying. She lost five pounds in there. Came out,
eyes bloodshot. Bags under here—

(ONE *continues speaking, but his voice drops out as* KEN
moves the microphone to TWO.)

TWO: My boyfriend injected into his penis and now he
has E D. Why would you inject anything into that? You
know how precious that is? You lose that, you have
to take it in the ass. That's the only sex you have. You
become a—

(TWO *continues speaking, his voice dropping out as* KEN
moves the microphone to THREE.)

THREE: Friday's my cheat day. I got a sesame bagel
with eggs. When I unwrapped it, it was an everything
bagel. I see poppy seeds. I have a new respect for
poppy seeds since they fucked with my tox screen last
year. Put my clock back to zero when I had eighty-nine
days clean. So I took it back to the guy and told him I
asked for a sesame bagel. He looked at me and started
scraping the eggs out. I said, "No, I need fresh eggs,
bacon, and cheese". Now the guy's pissed. He says,
"Oh, O K". Hands it back five minutes later. I take
a bite. It's crunchy. He scrambled the eggs with the
shells in. So I went out ordered French toast, went to
court, tested negative—

(THREE *continues and his voice drops out, as* KEN *hands the
microphone to* DENNIS.)

DENNIS: I thought I got chicken pox from eating
chicken nuggets. It was nothing—

(KEN *takes the microphone.* DENNIS *pulls it back.*)

DENNIS: And last night I had a good sleep. The past two years, falling asleep was like putting my finger in an electric socket. I was jumping. Jumping constantly. I thought the only way I'd ever sleep again was if you dropped a brick on my fucking head from six stories. Last night all I had to do was close my eyes.

(KEN *takes the microphone, and exits. The group members follow, leaving* DENNIS *alone on stage.*)

Scene 10

(KEN *enters and tosses* DENNIS *a blue ice pack.*)

KEN: Think fast.

(DENNIS *catches it.*)

DENNIS: Damn. That's gonna peel the skin off my hands.

KEN: It's important that it's cold. (*He arranges his chair four feet away from* DENNIS.) Follow my finger.

DENNIS: (*Dropping the ice pack*) What? This again?

KEN: We've only done it once.

DENNIS: That was enough. I'm cured.

KEN: Dennis, we only scratched the surface.

DENNIS: I told you, I got my head right now. It was confusing before. Like the radio when one station overlaps the other. I'm not confused with that other station no more.

KEN: You're doing better, but you know you can do better than this, Dennis. Don't slide back on me now.

DENNIS: I think I'm good.

(*Pause*)

KEN: You're going to be back with your daughter soon. Don't you want to be the best you can be for her?

(Pause)

DENNIS: O K, Chief.

(KEN places the ice pack in DENNIS' hands.)

DENNIS: What am I supposed to do with this?

KEN: Hold on to it. *(He moves his finger back and forth twenty times.)* What comes to mind?

(Three INSURGENTS appear behind KEN and DENNIS.)

DENNIS: I was with four guys. Good shooters. We were getting into some heavy stuff.

(With ice pack in hand, DENNIS runs for cover behind a dry wall panel. The INSURGENTS surround him.)

KEN: Stay there.

(DENNIS peeks from behind the wall, aiming the ice pack.)

DENNIS: They generals were like Crips and Bloods. Running up and down alleys shooting wild, just to get lucky. One guy came running toward us. He was smiling and waving a A K. I couldn't tell if he wanted to help us or kill us. He was holding a little girl in a sundress.

(An INSURGENT approaches DENNIS.)

KEN: Squeeze the ice pack. Feel how cold it is.

(DENNIS squeezes, triggering the sound of a gunshot. He aims the ice pack intently.)

DENNIS: We yelled at him to stop. Bullets was bouncing off the walls, and he kept moving the girl like to protect himself. She was crying. I remember her face expressions, everything. We said, "Drop the girl!" He kept coming, so we sprayed him.

(DENNIS *squeezes the ice pack again, triggering the sound of automatic rifle fire. The* INSURGENTS *retreat.*)

KEN: Can you still feel your fingers?

DENNIS: I'm getting numb.

KEN: Drop the ice pack.

(DENNIS *drops it.* KEN *does twenty more movements.*)

KEN: What do you get now?

DENNIS: There was blood pouring outta her. I took off my shirt and wrapped it around her head, but she was bleeding even more. (*He curls up his hands and blows on them for warmth.*)

KEN: That's right. Warm them up.

(DENNIS *starts rubbing his hands together.*)

DENNIS: I started praying. Our father. Who aren't in heaven. Hollow be thy name. The sun was still out. It was a funny light. Everything gold around me. I felt like I was looking at myself through a rifle scope backwards. My body was moving without me. My legs were all over the place. Left and right, and left and right, and a little bit advancing ahead. I think I had a heat stroke. Fireworks. I could see the side of the road, but it was agony to get there. I was making noise with my mouth. Oh my god. Oh no.

KEN: How are your hands?

DENNIS: Good. Tinkling. I need to throw up.

KEN: Notice that.

DENNIS: I sat on the side of the road and started digging her grave. (*He picks up a dry wall panel and rams it into the floor.*)

KEN: What are you thinking?

DENNIS: I'm pissed.

KEN: Stay with that.

DENNIS: I'm pissed that he put me in that position. I wasn't gonna turn around and run like a pussy. I had orders.

KEN: Pump your hands, Dennis.

(DENNIS *opens and closes his fists.*)

KEN: Feel the blood flowing through. *(Doing twenty more movements)* Stay with whatever's coming up.

(The LITTLE GIRL *in a sundress enters.* DENNIS *is transfixed.)*

DENNIS: The little girl is talking to me.

KEN: Keep breathing.

DENNIS: She wants me to come and see the moon. She's taking me by the hand. *(He wanders off.)*

KEN: What's the moon look like?

DENNIS: It has some stripes. It's like a watermelon and the white is very thick. Bigger than half. Very sharp. You have to look quick because it just disappears. *(He smiles.)*

KEN: Why are you smiling?

DENNIS: She likes the beads on my rosary. I buried it with her.

KEN: What do you feel right now?

DENNIS: I feel calmer. She knows.

KEN: What does she know?

DENNIS: It wasn't my fault. I couldn't protect her. I couldn't save her. But I wasn't using her as a human helmet. He was.

KEN: Is she still with you?

DENNIS: She's thanking me. She's telling me she has to go. She wants me to let her to rest.

(The LITTLE GIRL *exits.)*

KEN: How do you feel about that?

*(*DENNIS *returns to the chair and sits.)*

DENNIS: I feel like she's in God's hands now. I did everything what I could. *(Pause)* It's over.

KEN: Dennis, that's very good. You're not flooded by the memory. You stayed anchored in the present the whole time. That's exactly where we want you to be. Right here.

Scene 11

*(*FREDDY *joins* ALICE *in her cube.)*

FREDDY: I need your help. I got this letter from Dennis' lawyer. He's claiming the court is charging Dennis to have his record expunged, and that's extortion.

ALICE: Oh, Jesus Christ. Dennis was charged forty dollars per outpatient treatment. How is that extortion?

FREDDY: Can you talk to him?

ALICE: I talk to that ass every other week. He never listens. This is the person who's advising Dennis on legal matters. The person who thinks the court gets money from treatment centers. That we have a deal with the V A—we get kickbacks. I love it. We kept Dennis from doing jail time. We're cleaning his record. That's not enough. I guess he should have gone to jail and rotted in jail.

FREDDY: *(Quoting from the letter)* "At the plea bargain, at no time did he agree to issues of cost. Issues of cost did not arise until after the plea." What the fuck does that mean?

ALICE: It means he's an idiot. Dennis stopped throwing fits about his copays, I thought he was paying. No, on the advice of his clown college lawyer he has a bill for twelve hundred and eighty dollars with interest.

FREDDY: Well, this is a bag of dicks. Can it be forgiven?

ALICE: Hell no, he'll be on the hook for it until the day he dies. *(Pause)* Wait, does this mean Dennis' housing will fall through now?

FREDDY: Fuck if I'll let that happen. His housing is locked down. *(He exits.)*

Scene 12

(FREDDY visits DENNIS in the common area. DENNIS is preoccupied with a crossword puzzle booklet.)

FREDDY: You ready to get outta here?

DENNIS: I'm ready for a lot of things. I'm ready to get paid.

FREDDY: One more week. What are you doing to prepare?

DENNIS: Counselor Ken was a real push for me. He has me doing crossword puzzles and looking up the answers. Like the clue is "Ten commandments", and the answer is "Laws". I'm using it to learn vocabulary so I can socialize more.

FREDDY: You're not learning vocabulary.

DENNIS: What am I doing? The clue is "Toto's dog." I had forgot about Toto. I remember Toto.

FREDDY: You're learning crossword puzzle clues. That you can use to embrace the suck of this place and that's it. Once you get outta here, you wanna talk to people, invite 'em over to your place!

DENNIS: *(Too good to be true)* No.

FREDDY: The H U D voucher for your apartment came through.

DENNIS: The eagle shit that up for me?

FREDDY: I just went to see the building. The apartments are nice. All brand new. It has a kingsize bed.

DENNIS: Kingsize bed? What am I gonna do on a football field? I'll lose my legs and arms.

FREDDY: That's not all. If you're watching T V, a message will come on the screen telling you your laundry's ready.

DENNIS: Holy shit. I don't need all that.

FREDDY: You're getting it.

DENNIS: Does it have a room for my daughter? That's all I care about. According to those guidelines she needs to have her own room.

FREDDY: Roger that. It's a two bedroom. Ai-ee-yah!

Scene 13

(DENNIS *joins* ALICE *in her cube.*)

DENNIS: Am I coordinated?

ALICE: Looking good, Dennis.

DENNIS: Wanna see my socks? (*He raises his pantlegs.*)

ALICE: Tacos.

DENNIS: Nobody can even see them shits. I'm gonna be walking around like this. (*Raising his pantlegs and walking awkwardly*) I got blue on my shirt, blue in the taco. Yellow here and down there. (*Dropping his pants*) I have to walk out my house with an image. I'm a personal trainer. I'm advertising my own company.

ALICE: I got some news from the foster family that we need to discuss.

DENNIS: They're gonna be sailing the Caribbeans New Year's Eve?

ALICE: The foster family wants to adopt your daughter.

DENNIS: Look at the joke you pulling on me right now.

ALICE: It's not a joke.

(Pause)

DENNIS: How can they do that? Don't they gotta ask my permission?

ALICE: They're asking you and her mother to sign away your rights.

DENNIS: Sign away my what? I'm not giving away my daughter.

ALICE: Dennis—

DENNIS: And what they go to her ma for? That irks me.

ALICE: They need her consent, too.

DENNIS: Her ma would gave her consent to faces in the walls and shit. She worships the jaguar and eats psychedelic cactuses. She don't know what the fuck she doing! They take my baby, that's kidnapping. I'll be setting off Amber alarms.

ALICE: It's not kidnapping. It's a legal adoption.

DENNIS: I never put her up for adoption.

ALICE: Dennis, she hasn't been in your care for some time.

DENNIS: I'm still her father.

ALICE: Yes, you are. But this family has provided her with stability she didn't have.

DENNIS: What about my progress? I'm about to tell the judge I'm doing this, that, and the third. I have my housing. I'm clean. I finished my treatment. I made a con. I made a conscious effort to turn my life around.

ALICE: Do you have an income?

DENNIS: I'm a professional on exercises.

ALICE: But right now, you don't have an income. They don't wanna see you living off her checks.

DENNIS: I won't touch her checks. I know that's for her. Making on an income is the easiest thing to go through. Now that I got a little more straightforward in my life. I know I can hold my balance.

ALICE: If you wanna fight this, you can go that route, but it will be a hard road to go. *(Pause)* Do you think you'll have enough money to fight this?

DENNIS: My plan did not go past that deep. *(Pause)* Damn. What do these people want from me? I got nothing, so they get to keep my kid, too?

ALICE: Think about what looks best to Children and Youth Services. No one wanted Essie with her bloody little self giving everything MRSA. This family cleaned her up. She's healthy. She's enrolled in all kinds of lessons. She's with a family that can provide for her education, her future. And you. You've made amazing progress. But, objectively, you're a single father, with no support network, no income, and a debt of twelve jundred and eighty dollars to the treatment centers.

DENNIS: Child Services don't know shit about me! The judge plays favorites to them! Who the fuck are they? A buncha white girls in they first job outta college! It's the first time people care what they have to say. They go crazy with power snatching people's kids. Someone oughtta kick they ass!

ALICE: You're right. They make a lot of assumptions. And that translates to people like you not being given a break.

DENNIS: Why can't the judge see through that shit? He's like a horse. *(Shielding his eyes with horse blinders)* He can't see beyond this line or that line. I live every momit for that kid. I could chose to keep a distant. I didn't. I saw her four hours every week. Everything I did was for her. The judge should see that.

ALICE: I'm sorry, Dennis.

DENNIS: This is beyond the borderline of what's right, Miss Alice.

ALICE: I agree with you. You don't deserve to lose your kid. I just don't want you to go up against a losing battle. *(Pause)* It's up to you. You need to make the decision that's right for you and Essie. Only you know what that is.

Scene 14

(The park. MARCO enters hula hooping. DENNIS hangs from a chin-up bar; he jumps down.)

DENNIS: You have to learn a nice way to hula hoop. You hula hoop violently. You hold your breath.

MARCO: What's the point of the hula hoop?

DENNIS: The strength. The abdomen. The legs. It's gonna fall a number of times. It helps your heart. *(He demonstrates with the hula hoop.)* Now I can do this, and it's smooth.

MARCO: We gonna run laps now?

DENNIS: You wanna run, do that on your time. But stay off the track.

MARCO: Why?

DENNIS: Don't run on anything hard. Look for something that lives. *(He drops the hula hoop and picks up an elastic resistance cord. He tucks the cord under his*

feet and pulls the handles up to his chest.) Watch. The legs
are supposed to be a circle for the energy to move.
That's why people have bow legs, some of them. With
pumping iron, you stop: it goes away. This one, it lasts
forever. Inside the body. It's an energy. It moves. It
tinkles. It's not Tai Chi. It's Tai Chi Chung.

MARCO: Wow, I got a physical trainer and a lunatic at
the same time. Bargain.

DENNIS: Who you calling a lunatic in those sunglasses,
Papo?

MARCO: I lost two pairs of good sunglasses. These ugly
ones are always in front of my face. Couldn't lose 'em
if I tried.

DENNIS: Go.

(MARCO tries the exercise.)

MARCO: Tell me something. How you call yourself a
trainer if you don't follow a diet? You eat fast food all
the time.

DENNIS: I know mad shit on proteins. Now shut your
mouth and hold it for three seconds. That's when it
does the work.

MARCO: I like weights better. You can switch to heavier
ones.

DENNIS: It's not the heavier weights, it's the repetitions
that matter. Straighten your arms, push your
shoulders up. If it's hurting a lot here, you doing it
wrong. Twenty times, every movement. You have
to be repetitious about it to strengthen the muscle.
Lifting heavier weights, you injure. You taking steps
backwards. Do you have any trapezius problems?

MARCO: What?

DENNIS: *(Showing where)* More commonly known as:
back. We do rowing for that. This shit is lethal.

(DENNIS *demos rowing.* MARCO *follows suit with a comical lack of aptitude.*)

DENNIS: Now that we're down here. Let's do the stabilizer.

MARCO: More commonly known as: Xanax.

(DENNIS *demos crunches.*)

MARCO: Hold on. (*He wipes his brow, and takes off his light jacket. He has another light jacket on underneath. He takes that off, and is down to a hoodie.*)

DENNIS: Damn. You have five outfits on top.

MARCO: It was supposed to be colder. (*He attempts the crunches; he succumbs to a side-stitch early on.*)

DENNIS: We getting those heat waves. Even in winter. The same weather with the Sahara in Egypt. Globalization is also with the weather. It's all gonna be one. One weather across all countries. And it's hot. Civilization did all that. Going to the moon. Digging for whatever. We running out of water. You interfere with everything. The oil zone don't exist no more. What did we accomplish going up there? Looking for another planet. People are starving here.

MARCO: Good workout, Dennis. Add this to my tab, O K?

DENNIS: You said you were paying me what you owed me today.

MARCO: Rough week. I don't have the cash.

DENNIS: Fuck! I ain't doing this for free, Papo.

MARCO: I know you're not and I want to pay you. Listen, Suski docked my last two checks.

DENNIS: You shoulda cancelled! I coulda been working with someone else who would paid me.

MARCO: You told me I was your only client. I wanted to support you.

DENNIS: Well, you're wack. You're messing with my lifelihood. I was counted on the sixty bucks. I have a cawta.

MARCO: A quarter?

DENNIS: Cota, man! A fucking cota, and shit ain't working out! I didn't even get five people this month. *(About resistance tubes)* I paid two hundred dollars for these rubberbands.

MARCO: I'm sure more clients will meet you in the park and pay cash.

DENNIS: Where the fuck do I find 'em? Advertising or some shit? How much that cost?

MARCO: Don't pay for advertising. You just need more testimonials. Word of mouth takes patience.

DENNIS: I can't take the patience. I got no other money coming in.

MARCO: What happened to Bally's?

DENNIS: The manager at Bally's started having verbal words with me because I didn't give them a procentage for using their gym, so they kicked me out.

MARCO: Shit. What about your hearing coming up?

DENNIS: *(Pause; lost in thought)* The judge won't mind that. He's pretty understandable. He'll be happy I'm starting my own business.

Scene 15

(DENNIS joins ALICE in her cube.)

ALICE: Her mother signed.

DENNIS: No lie to that. If you could list all the good qualities in a person: brains, beauty, nature, fairness. She got none of 'em. What you expect?

ALICE: Yep.

DENNIS: I'm glad Essie don't take after her footprints.

ALICE: Dennis, have you made a decision?

DENNIS: I don't know what to do. I feel like I might have a real fall back.

ALICE: Have you spoken to your lawyer?

DENNIS: He told me to fight it if I want.

ALICE: Don't listen to your lawyer. He's trying to make money.

DENNIS: Who should I listen to?

ALICE: Yourself. What do you think?

DENNIS: (Getting upset) Miss Alice, she's my baby. Fuck.

ALICE: What?

DENNIS: I can't say it. If I say it, I might bust outta my clothes and turn into a green hawk.

ALICE: Well, I'd like to see that.

DENNIS: You bout to.

ALICE: Go ahead.

DENNIS: I can't give her all what she needs.

ALICE: O K. That's a big deal to say that.

DENNIS: No matter what I do, I fuck it up!

ALICE: No, you don't. You're not fucking this up. I can think of a million ways you could fuck this up that you aren't. You're not thinking about yourself, you're thinking about Essie. That's what real fathers do. I'm proud of you, Dennis. You're good.

(Pause)

DENNIS: What happens if I sign?

ALICE: The adoption goes forward.

DENNIS: No, I mean does it got a sentence in there that I can't see Essie no more?

ALICE: No, you can still see her. They want you to be in her life. You can still have regular contact and see her grow up.

(Pause)

DENNIS: O K. I'll sign.

(Nightmare 4)

(The sound of the screaming demon. The LITTLE GIRL *appears in a fancier dress, and fancier shoes.)*

DENNIS: Essie. They chosed you. I'm so proud. You got something every kid wants. Some kind of security of family. A family to fall back on later in life. A family to look forward to. A family that can see the potentials in you, so you'll be able to fill your dreams. Come here.

(The LITTLE GIRL *runs toward* DENNIS.*)*

DENNIS: I remember when you were a baby. You were progressing. Saying words. You said, "Bubbles". You were pointing. You started to walk. You were awkward. You tried, you falled. I said, "Get up". You looked. I said, "Get up! If you don't, I'll pop you on the butt!" Come here.

*(*DENNIS *embraces the* LITTLE GIRL.*)*

DENNIS: You'll always be my nena.

*(*LITTLE GIRL *slips out of* DENNIS'*s arms and exits.)*

END OF PLAY

www.ingramcontent.com/pod-product-compliance
Lightning Source LLC
Chambersburg PA
CBHW070028110426
42741CB00034B/2680